Read with Me ... Again

niace

promoting adult learning

© National Institute of Adult Continuing Education, 2010
Published by NIACE, 21 De Montfort Street, Leicester, LE1 7GE

LOOK AT YOU!
Text © 2006 Kathy Henderson. Illustrations © 2006 Paul Howard
Reproduced by permission of Walker Books Ltd, London

SHOE BABY
Text © 2005 Joyce Dunbar. Illustrations © 2005 Polly Dunbar
Reproduced by permission of Walker Books Ltd, London

SLEEPY PLACES
Text © 2006 Judy Hindley. Illustrations © 2006 Tor Freeman
Reproduced by permission of Walker Books Ltd, London

GINGER FINDS A HOME
Copyright © 2003 Charlotte Voake
Reproduced by permission of Walker Books Ltd, London

ISBN: 978-1-86201-437-4

Read with Me ... Again

T his is a second book for parents and carers who want to read with their children. The first *Read with Me* was produced by the Basic Skills Agency (BSA) and bought by thousands of schools and parents. We had so many people telling us how popular it was that we decided, when the BSA merged with NIACE, to produce a follow-up.

Parents and other adults have an essential part to play in giving children a love of reading and an interest in books which will give them a strong foundation for their education. We hope that the advice in both *Read with Me* books will give you the confidence and enthusiasm to read regularly with your children and start them off on a lifetime of pleasure in reading.

This book includes four delightful stories by authors whose books are loved by children and grown-ups all over the world. I would like to thank Kathy Henderson and Paul Howard, Judy Hindley and Tor Freeman, Joyce and Polly Dunbar, Charlotte Voake, and their publisher Walker Books for granting permission for us to use their stories. I'm sure you and your children will enjoy them.

Carol Taylor
Director of Operations, NIACE

Introduction

WELCOME to *Read with Me ... Again!*

This book is full of ideas for helping your child to read and enjoy books. It's for parents and other grown-ups who are willing to find time to share books and stories with their young children.

We all want to help our children with reading, but we may not be sure how to go about it. We may think that teachers are the best people to help a child with reading and that parents should not interfere. But parents, carers and other adults can instil a love of reading long before a child goes to school and deepen that love of reading as a child grows up.

Enjoyment of books is the most important factor when learning to read.

Sharing books with adults helps children with learning to read.

This book is not about teaching your child to read. It's about creating situations where books and reading are associated with happy times. Children who know that reading brings pleasure are more likely to become lifelong readers. In this book you will find four stories by authors enjoyed by many young children. Each story is surrounded by guidance which will help you to make the story more enjoyable for your child. Look at the suggestions and decide which ones you would like to use. They are not a list of instructions, but ideas to try out.

The stories have many features loved by children – rhythm, rhyme, repetition and the element of surprise. In the widest sense, all four books are about being looked after and cared for. They offer opportunities for adults and children to talk about and share experiences and events in a reassuring and comforting way.

The golden rules

* Make reading a time of pleasure for you both.

* Start sharing books even before your child knows which way up to hold the book – from birth!

* Accept your child's efforts with praise.

* Read books your child loves.

* Focus on the things that are right, not the mistakes.

* Keep reading to children even after they've learned to read independently.

* Stop when they've had enough – it's not a punishment!

For some children, learning to read will seem to happen easily and quickly. For others, more time and support will be needed. Whatever the case, your help will be a powerful influence over your child's development as a reader. For **all** children, praise, encouragement, reassurance and pleasure are the vital factors towards becoming a confident reader.

Getting started

Reading with babies to 3-year-olds

Babies see objects and distinguish shapes and colours from a very early age. They love to share books with adults and enjoy the closeness of looking at books, hearing rhymes and jingles, being involved in actions or feeling textures. It's important to start early because it sets the scene for later development. And it's a lot of fun for adults as well as babies.

- Look for cloth books that can safely be chewed, and that can be washed.

- Share board books that have only a few pages.

- Collect books that won't get damaged – if they get wet in the bath, for instance, or in your baby's mouth.

- Read with your baby often – and let babies see you reading too.

- Snuggle up with their favourite blanket or toy and then look at the book together.

- Choose a book with only a few – or no – words in it, talk about the pictures and tell your baby what's in them.

- Don't feel embarrassed if you think you're talking to yourself and you feel silly – it's just what they need.

- The more books you share, the better your baby will be at learning to communicate – just watch the smiles and laughter as you read favourites again and again.

- Sing rhymes and jingles too, and help your baby to join in with the actions. 'Round and round the garden, like a teddy bear' and 'This little piggy went to market' always make babies laugh.

- If you're not sure about what rhymes and jingles to use, or which books to read with your baby, ask your local library about parent and baby sessions.

- Booktrust provides free books for babies and when your baby is three months old or so, you will be given the first of a set of free books. Your child will get another set at three and then five years of age.

- Libraries provide free books, too. It's never too early to join.

- Enjoy the fun of sharing books with your baby, and remember to do so a little at a time and often so it's something to look forward to.

- Set up the routine of reading a bedtime story – then it can continue throughout childhood and beyond.

Reading with 3 to 5-year-olds

At this stage, children should learn that books are a pleasure. They need to handle books, enjoy the pictures and hear lots of stories of rhymes. This is not the time to worry about testing them on the words they know or sounding out words. Just enjoy the time you spend together sharing books. This will give children the best foundation for learning to read and love books. Grandparents and big brothers and sisters can be part of this too.

- Read to your child as often as possible – any time, any place, anywhere – in bed, in the car, in the bath. Also, try to keep a special time for reading when you can cuddle up together.

- Bring stories to life with lots of expression and silly voices.

- Talk about stories and pictures and play 'Guess what's going to happen next'.

- Read favourite books over and over again. You might have had enough of reading *Three Little Pigs* or *Chicken Licken* but young children love familiarity.

- Say the catchy bits together, e.g. 'Run, run as fast as you can', 'He huffed and he puffed and he blew the house down!'

- Learn rhymes, songs and jingles together so you both know them by heart and can point to the words as you recite them together.

- Encourage your child to bring books home from nursery or school and make the time to read them together.

- Buy books if you can. Boot sales are a good place for bargains. Put them around the house in baskets and boxes – like a lucky dip your child can choose from.

- Go to the library – the books are free and they have a great selection for children. Librarians love babies and children who love books.

- Play a game of 'spot the words' on signs and labels – on the street, in shops and in your cupboards.

- Make sure your child sees you reading newspapers, books and magazines – show them it's cool to read.

Becoming independent

Reading with 5 to 6-year-olds

This is the stage when children can tell you about their favourite story and when they begin to pick out well-known words or phrases, e.g. 'Once upon a time', 'In a dark, dark wood'.

- Take turns to read bits of a favourite story. A whole story is too daunting for the reader. Don't worry if your child has memorised words or phrases. This is an important part of learning to read. It gives a sense of satisfaction and is not cheating. Recognising words will soon follow once the story is familiar.

- Talk about pictures and details that catch your child's interest. This will help with understanding the story and with guessing new words. Guessing is important when the child understands what the story is likely to say and choose words which make sense.

- Run your finger under the words as you read together. In this way, words are seen and heard together.

- Don't make a fuss if your child can't read a word. Either say the word yourself or encourage your child to think about what it might say. Draw attention to the starting sound of the word. Don't get cross. At this stage it is more important that your child enjoys sharing stories than getting every word right.

- Play alphabet and sound games such as 'I spy'. Children learn a lot about words, letters and sounds through these simple games.

- Continue to read to your child every day.

- Write notes or text messages to your child – it's a great way to get them to focus on words.

Reading with 6 to 7-year-olds

At this stage many children want some independence and to read on their own. But they'll still want quiet times with you to share the books they love or to hear you read more challenging material.

* **Keep reading together – every day if possible. Take turns to read to each other.**

* Show you are really interested in finding out what happens in the story. Talk about beginnings and endings; the characters and how they behave; the bits you find sad, funny or exciting; the words and pictures you find interesting.

* Encourage interest in a wide range of material by reading aloud from newspapers or magazines and by drawing attention to snippets which the children might like to read. Help your child choose a range of books from the library.

* Tell each other about your favourite books and recognise that you may have quite different ideas about what you'd like to read. Respect each other's preferences and choices.

Babies to 3-year-olds

Look at you! Wow, what a body can do!

By Kathy Henderson, illustrated by Paul Howard

This is a delightful book that just captures the 'baby-ness' of babies. The pictures show all kinds of babies with all kinds of adults and some older children too. Everyday activities such as eating, nappy-changing, bathing, playing and sleeping are shown with a few words to describe them, in large print. It's an ideal book to share with toddlers, as well as babies, and lends itself wonderfully to bouncing, tickling and cuddling as you go!

Guidelines

This book has 32 pages, but there's no need to read them all in one sitting. It's fine to dip in and out and just look at a bit at a time.

The following suggestions follow the pages of the book, but it's perfectly all right to use them in any order.

You can do the activities over and over again, especially the ones your baby likes.

LOOK at YOU!

WOW, WHAT A BODY CAN DO!

Kathy Henderson
Illustrated by Paul Howard

Fingers and toes wiggle.
Eyes, nose and mouth giggle.
Arms wave, legs kick …
bottoms squirm …
and tummies tickle.

Clothes on.
Where's the baby gone?
There he is!
Clothes off!
Where are the baby's toes?
There they are!

- The background colours on the pages in the story will help you to break it up into 'chunks' or very small chapters.

- Each chunk starts with a letter that has a coloured background too.

- Find somewhere cosy and comfortable to snuggle up and make sure it's as quiet as possible, so turn off the TV or the radio so they don't distract either you or your baby.

- You can choose whether all the babies in the books are boys or girls and you can give them names if you want to – one of them could be your baby and have the same name!

- Show your baby the front cover and point to the picture of a happy baby.

- Point to his eyes, nose, teeth, tongue, chin, arms, hands, fingers, etc.

- As you turn the pages to get to the start of the story, you'll see the same picture from the cover again and the words 'Look at you!'

Reading with your child

- The first chunk of the book is four pages long and each page has a blue background. The first word, Fingers, has a pink background around the letter 'F'. You could look at this bit by itself.

- The words make a little jingle – read them all as you look at the pictures:

  Fingers and toes wiggle.

  Eyes, nose and mouth giggle.

  Arms wave, legs kick...

  bottoms squirm...

  and tummies tickle.

- Talk about the pictures separately.

- There are pictures of dogs and babies and bubbles in the book. Point to them, and tell your baby that they're having fun looking and laughing at bubbles.

- Then look for the dog sleeping with a baby leaning against it and the blue teddy next to the recliner chair.

- Talk about the toddler tickling the baby and do the same where your baby enjoys being tickled.

- The next four pages are all about getting dressed and they have a pink background, with a green background for the first letter of 'Clothes'.

Lie, roll, sit, *wobble*.
Rock, crawl, pull, *wobble*.
Stand, *wobble*, sway, *wobble*.
Bump! Step, walk, *toddle*!

What can you see?
Something to eat.
What can you hear?
A song in the air.
What can you smell?
mmmmm! Food.

How does it taste? Good,
good, good.
And how does it feel?
Warm and squelchy, scratchy,
rough, sticky, squishy …
Time for a bath!

Float, soap, splash, wash,
slide, glide, cuddle, brush.

Clip, snip, some things
grow quick.
Hey ho, others grow slow!

Funny thing hair …
You can brush it this way,
you can brush it that,
wash it, dry it, tie it up and
squash it flat.
I feel …
good, bad, happy, sad,
bold, shy (I don't
know why).

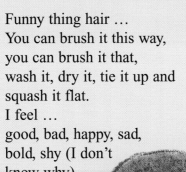

- Look at the way the words rhyme and read them as a sort of game to include your baby as you go.

  Clothes on.

  Where's the baby gone?

  There he is!

  Clothes off!

  Where are the baby's toes?

  There they are!

- You will probably remember this the more you read it and you can say it as you dress and undress your baby.

- Point out the T-shirt, nappy and socks, and compare them with your baby's clothes.

- Talk about how the mummy is looking after the baby and how he likes what's happening to him.

- The four pages with a green background are all about babies moving and exploring the space around them and going through the stages of learning to walk from being born and lying still.

- The emphasis is on the word 'wobble', so you could wobble your baby as you say it each time:

  Lie, roll, sit, *wobble*.

  Rock, crawl, pull, *wobble*.

  Stand, wobble, sway, *wobble*.

  Bump! Step, walk, **toddle**!

- Talk about how this is what your baby will do and if you have a toddler as well, tell her that this is just what she did from being a tiny baby.

- Food and eating are the next themes of the book and they have an olive green background with images of lots of babies waiting for food and then eating it.

- Use the rhymes when your baby is actually eating and repeat the phrases as she is in her high chair.

- Talk about the senses of seeing, hearing, smelling, tasting and feeling, then point to your baby's eyes, ears, nose, mouth and fingers as you read these pages.

- The book continues in similar ways through bath time, with blue backgrounds to the pages; the growth of hair, nails and new babies, on a grey background; to emotions and learning to get along with other children.

I want yours!
No! It's mine!
I feel lonely.
I feel fine.

A-a-a-chooo!
Wow! What a body can do!
Yawn! Hic! Plenty of tricks.
Whoops! Pooh!
Wow! What a body can do!

Sigh, flop, snuggle down,
curl up in a heap.
The story's done, this
body's tired and now it's
going to sleep.

- Each of these chunks can be used separately and you will find all kinds of ways to play with the words, show your baby the pictures and talk about how they all relate to you and your family.

- The final sections of the book deal with what the baby's body can do, such as sneezing, yawning, hiccupping and needing a nappy change, before the end pages, which describe tiredness, going to bed and falling asleep.

- You could talk about these and use them at bedtime as well as other times during the day when your baby has a rest.

- Look at the pictures together and tell your baby about making friends, sharing things, playing and starting to see what others do and join in with new activities.

- This could be at times when you visit toddler groups or go to the health centre or the library.

- Enjoy all the many babies and their typical days and relate them to your own and your baby's routines.

3 to 5-year-olds

Shoe Baby

By Joyce Dunbar, illustrated by Polly Dunbar

Shoe baby *tells the tale of the adventures of a baby on land, in the air and on the sea, before he is returned safely to his mother and father. The story is told in a lively, rhythmic verse which may well remind you and your child of other rhymes that you know. The illustrations are richly detailed and full of jokes and surprises to share.*

Guidelines

Read through the suggestions and choose the ones that appeal to you and your child. Be prepared to read and share the book over and over again! Remember, these are only suggestions, what you do and say should be guided by what your child notices, says and asks, and will develop as you both become more familiar with the story. The rhyme and repetition will help your child – but don't forget to examine and talk about the pictures.

- **Hold the book together and look at the cover. What can you see? Does the baby look happy or sad?**

Joyce Dunbar
Illustrated by Polly Dunbar

There was once a baby
Who hid in a shoe
And had learnt how to say,
"How do you do?"

In a shoe you might think
There is not much to do,
But this very same baby
Went to SEA in that shoe!

A dolphin came by
And an octopus too.
Said this sail-away baby
"How do you do?"

And this baby I tell you
Went to TOWN in that shoe,
Passing the shops
On the way to the zoo.

At the monkeys he waved
And the elephants too
And he greeted them all
With a "How do you do?"

This very same baby
FLEW in that shoe!
To the birds of the air he said
"How do you do?"

Then this fly-away baby
SANG in the shoe.
"Dum-de-dum. Tra-la-la.
How do you do?"

Later this baby
Had TEA in that shoe
He invited the Queen
Who brought the King too.

"Good gracious!" they said,
"Pray who are you?"
With a bow said the baby,
"How do you do?"

At long last this baby
Slept in that shoe
So dozy, so cosy,
So tickety-boo.

And he dreamed a bright dream
Of a pink cockatoo
Saying over and over
"Toodle-oo! Toodle-oo!"

- Take your time to turn the pages – share what you see as you go.

- On the opening page of the story point to the shoes and talk about them. How many? What colours? What patterns? Which do you like best?

- When you read, emphasise the rhyme.

- Read 'How do you do?' in a way that will be memorable and enjoyable – for example, the deep voice of an educated adult – because it is going to be repeated regularly throughout the story.

- Point to the people and creatures that the baby meets. What do you notice about them?

- Look at and talk about what the shoe becomes at different times in the story – how it changes to suit the situation.

- Talk about how the baby looks on all these adventures.

- Emphasise the rhyme and slow down to encourage your child to join in with 'How do you do?'

- Over time, encourage your child to anticipate 'How do you do?'

Reading with your child

- Match your reading to the change in the story when we meet the giants – slower and sadder. Your child may well have met giants in other stories – but make sure they understand about their size.

- Emphasise words like 'Stamping and shouting' and 'Sobbing and sighing'.

- Read 'BOO-HOO-HOO!' loudly.

- Point to the words 'BOO-HOO-BOO!' and encourage your child to join in.

- Talk about what we notice about the giant's feet.

- Ask your child how we know the giantess is sad and why she is sad.

- Point out how the words grow as the baby grows out of the shoe. Use your voice to emphasise the growth.

- Talk about how the giants look and feel when they find their baby (and the shoe!).

But now … there's a noise …
"BOO-HOO-HOO!
BOO-HOO-HOO!"
And a giant comes by
Wearing only one shoe.

And he makes such a fuss
Such a hullabaloo,
Stamping and shouting,
"WHO TOOK MY SHOE?"

And following fast
Came a giantess too,
Sobbing and sighing,
"BOO-HOO-HOO!
BOO-HOO-HOO!"

And into her polka-dot
hankie she blew,
"My baby! He's lost!
Oh what shall I do?"

All at once this strange baby
Grew in the shoe.
He grew and he grew
Right out of that shoe!

"Peekaboo!" said the baby,
Popping up from the shoe
"Hey Papa! Hey Mama!
How do you do?"

My shoe," said Papa.
"My runaway shoe!
I could find only one,
But now I have two!"

"My baby," said Mama.
"It really is you!
High and low have I looked
But not in a shoe!"

And the baby just beamed
and said,
"How do you do?"

- 'Peekaboo' is a word your child may well be familiar with from games you've played. Talk about why the baby says 'Peekaboo'.

- In the final picture, talk about the size of the giants, compared to the buildings.

- Who else do we see in the final picture?

- Each time you re-read the story, expect and make space for your child to join in – and even take over at times!

5 to 6-year-olds

Sleepy Places

By Judy Hindley, illustrated by Tor Freeman

Sleepy Places, *as the title suggests, is all about going to sleep – but where? It is an engaging story, which satisfyingly, ends in sleep. It is told in a gentle, rhythmic rhyme. It has delightful illustrations which will surprise and amuse you and your child if you look carefully enough! The words invite and prompt your child and you to respond and to join in.*

Judy Hindley
Illustrated by Tor Freeman

When you're yawning and nodding and flopping,
and ready to fall in a heap,
where do you choose for a nap or a snooze
– where is your favourite place to sleep?

A rabbit sleeps tight in its burrow;
a bird snuggles down in a tree.
A frog takes a snooze in the ooze of a pond;
a rose makes a bed for a bee.

Do you suppose you could drowse in a rose,
or snooze in the ooze like a frog?

A cat can nap on somebody's hat;
a bear curls up in a cave.

A fish may dream in the reeds of a stream;
a seal lolls about on a wave …

Can you imagine what dreams you'd have,
lolling about on a wave?

A swift can sleep on the wing as it flies;
a horse can sleep on the hoof;
bats hang upside down from their toes,
in rows upon rows in the roof.

If you were a bat, you'd sleep like that,
upside down in the roof!

Guidelines

Read through the suggestions and choose the ones you think are most appropriate for you and your child. This is a book that your child is likely to want to share over and over again, so be prepared to adapt and extend the ideas to suit yourselves.

- **Talk about the cover and the title page. Share your ideas about what's happening.**

- **Read the opening verse in a gentle and rhythmic way.**

- **Talk about your favourite place to sleep.**

- **Look at the detail of the picture – ask your child what they notice about the children. (The children appear in many of the illustrations.)**

Reading with your child

- There is plenty to notice and talk about in each picture. Ask your child what they notice in the picture of the creatures sleeping (rabbit, bird, frog and bee) apart from the fact that they are asleep.

- Emphasise the rhythm and rhyme – especially 'snooze' and 'ooze'.

- Encourage your child to anticipate some of the rhymes.

- Emphasise and talk about the words that suggest tiredness – 'yawning', 'nodding', 'flopping'; and those that suggest sleep – 'drowse', 'snooze', 'nap'. Can you think of any other sleepy words?

- Repeat the earlier activity – ask your child what they notice in the picture of the creatures sleeping (cat, bear, fish, seal; swift, horse and bats; pups and kangaroos).

A pup likes to sleep in a quivering heap,
With a bundle of sisters and brothers.

Kangaroo joeys tuck themselves up
in pockets attached to their mothers.

But what about you?
What place do you choose
– what sleepy place for a
nap or a snooze?

A nest of cushions,
a cave of quilts,
a bundle of pillows …
a cot, a pram?
A hammock, a sofa, a box, a rug, a comfy lap, a cuddly arm?

Or would you choose your own little bed?
With your own little blanket and pillow,
and kisses and stories and teddies and things,
and somebody tucking you in?

Oh yes – we each have a favourite sleepy place …
Goodnight. Goodnight. Goodnight!

- Look at the picture that suggests what the fish might be dreaming about – talk about your dreams and your child's dreams.

- Talk about the way the children appear and re-appear in some of the pictures.

- Once they are familiar with the story, encourage your child to read some of the lines.

- Talk about some of the places where you and your child have fallen asleep.

- Talk about some strange places where you would like to fall asleep!

6 to 7-year-olds

Ginger Finds a Home

By Charlotte Voake

Ginger is a street cat without much hope in his life. But one day, his prospects change when a little girl befriends him and his future starts to look a lot better. This is exactly the kind of story that would appeal to a child who has just begun to read independently. The illustrations are wonderful, the print large enough and well-spaced on the page so as not to be intimidating, and the story will appeal to all age groups – and adults too.

Guidelines

- **Read the book with your child in a quiet, comfy place that you both like.**

- **Point out the pictures of Ginger and how sad he looks, then talk about what it's like to feel unwanted and unloved.**

- **Look together at the words and run your finger under them as you read. Your child might join in some of them as you go.**

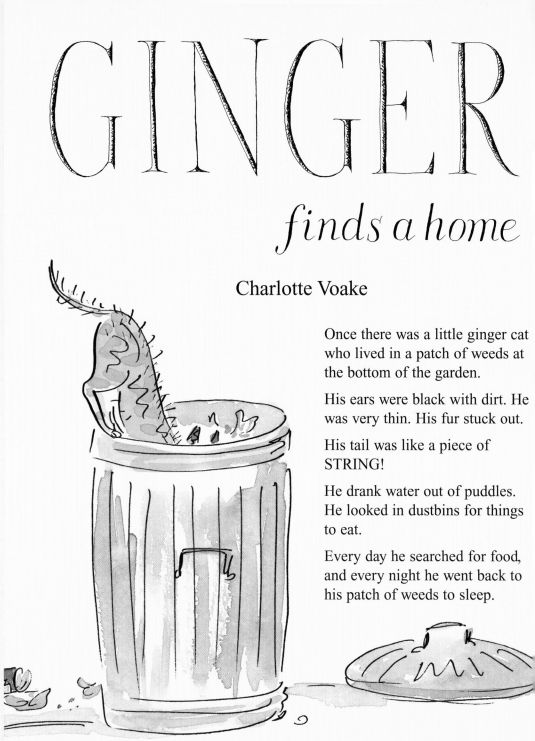

GINGER
finds a home

Charlotte Voake

Once there was a little ginger cat who lived in a patch of weeds at the bottom of the garden.

His ears were black with dirt. He was very thin. His fur stuck out.

His tail was like a piece of STRING!

He drank water out of puddles. He looked in dustbins for things to eat.

Every day he searched for food, and every night he went back to his patch of weeds to sleep.

Then one day, everything changed.

The little cat had found nothing to eat except a bit of bread, and he was cold and hungry as he came back to bed.

He stopped. There on the ground was …

a delicious plate of cat food!

He couldn't believe his eyes!

He gobbled it up and went to sleep. He had never slept so well!

The next night, he found another plate of food waiting for him …

and SOMETHING ELSE.

A little girl!

"Hello," she said.

She tried to stroke his fur, but he was frightened, and ran to hide in the weeds.

"See you tomorrow," said the little girl.

She came to visit him every day.

She bought him lovely things to eat.

She called him Ginger.

- **Talk about how Ginger lives from day to day and doesn't know how he will eat or what will happen to him from morning until night, and share sympathy for his plight.**

- **Look at the pictures and talk about cats outside, in the neighbourhood, your own cat perhaps, or those belonging to people you know.**

- **Share your feelings about how important it is to look after others, how you look after your child, how they care about people and animals too.**

- **You could ask what it feels like to have food regularly and what it might be like if this didn't happen.**

- **As you get further into the story, to the part where the little girl makes friends with Ginger, you could talk about your child's friends and how important they are.**

- **You might discuss what friendship means and how you can make new friends.**

- **Fear becomes an important theme as the story progresses, both of physical things and also of emotional loss leading to sadness.**

Reading with your child

- Use this part of the book to draw out any feelings and thoughts your child might have about their emotions or things that frighten or worry them.

- When you have finished the story for the first time, be prepared to read it many times over again. As you re-read, point to the words and ask your child to share the reading with you.

- If they struggle with a word, just tell them what it is and with practice, they will read it correctly.

- If they don't read the words exactly accurately but get the meaning right, for example, if they say 'chairs' instead of 'furniture' when Ginger runs and hides in the house, don't worry. This means that they understand the story and want to make it work for them. You can point out the right words later.

Soon Ginger looked forward to seeing the little girl. He came when she called, and when she stroked him, he purred.

The little girl loved Ginger.

"Ginger," she said. "You can't stay here. Why don't you come home with me?"

So Ginger followed the little girl home.

He had never been in a house before.

He looked in all the corners and under all the furniture. But poor Ginger was so nervous …

that when the little girl tried to shut the door,

he ran out into the garden as fast as he could.

The little girl looked outside. She couldn't see him anywhere. "Ginger!" she called.

But Ginger didn't come.

"I've frightened him away," she said. "He doesn't want to live with me."

The little girl was very sad. She was so upset, she didn't notice …

- As their confidence grows, and with your support, your child should manage some and then all of the reading alone and independently.

- You could then find other books to share together by the same author or look for stories about similar themes.

- Don't forget to keep encouraging your child to carry on reading and enjoying books.

when Ginger came creeping back in.

"Miaow!" said Ginger.

"GINGER!" said the little girl.

Now Ginger lives with the little girl in her house.

He is a very happy cat.

And the only time he ever goes back to the patch of weeds at the bottom of the garden …

is to sunbathe!

Parent questions

When should I start reading with my child?

It's never too early to read to your child or to sing songs and rhymes. Babies and toddlers enjoy looking at picture books and hearing stories read aloud. They love the rhythms and patterns of familiar stories and rhymes, as well as the pleasure of snuggling up to parents or grandparents.

What sort of text should I read to my child?

Anything that you feel happy to read – rhymes, picture books, folk tales, information books, comics, signs, labels, or sports reports from the newspaper. Children love the experience of sitting close to you and hearing your voice, and if you are enjoying what you are reading, they are learning that reading is a pleasure.

What if they want the same book over and over again?

Let them have it. Children love favourite stories. Through rereading, they learn the patterns of written language, and that reading is an enjoyable experience. Just make sure that you also introduce new stories to give them a taste of something different.

When should I ask my child to take part in reading?

Most children have a favourite story. When reading a story that is familiar to your child, leave gaps and you will find that they will finish the ends of sentences or join in with repeated phrases, e.g. 'Run, run as fast as you can' or 'Fee, fi, fo, fum'. This is the beginning of reading, although your child is 'reading' from memory. Once a child is familiar with the story, they can then begin to recognise the words in print. At this stage, children may choose to take the book and 'tell' the story in their own words.

What about the alphabet?

Encourage your child to learn letter names and letter sounds. Children need easy familiarity with letters to recognise their shape and talk about them by name. Alphabet friezes and plastic letters help children learn the names of letters. Games such as 'I-Spy' or silly sentences, rhyming games and songs help children hear letter sounds or word patterns.

What if my child makes a mistake?

If the 'mistake' makes sense, let your child continue reading. The mistakes that matter are the ones that don't make sense. It's helpful to read the last two sentences again. Include the word your child used. Talk about whether it makes sense. Tell your child the correct word. The most important thing when reading is that the meaning is clear.

What should I do if my child doesn't recognise a word?

In the early stages, just say the word to keep the meaning of the story, or quietly say the first sound and see if your child can predict what the word is. Don't ask your child to sound out an unknown word as this generally doesn't work, particularly with small, common words such as 'the', 'this', 'you'. If in doubt, always tell your child the word.

Should I cover up the pictures?

No, pictures are full of interest to children and give clues about what is happening in a story. Encourage your child to look closely at the pictures, to help them with their predictions.

How often should my child read to me?

Encourage your child to read to you a few times each week at a time that suits you both. They may also like to read to a younger brother or sister, or to grandparents. If your child gets tired, always finish the story and chat about what you've read.

How can I help when my child wants to read silently?

If your child prefers to read silently, particularly as they read longer stories, just chat about their view of the story or the style of the author or the illustrator. Continue to show that you are interested in their choice but respect their growing independence as readers. It is important, however, to continue to read aloud to your child, whatever their stage of reading development.

What next?

Helping your child learn to read, and making sure that reading is an ongoing part of their life, is a long process. You don't have to struggle with this on your own. There are lots of people and organisations that can help you with information and ideas.

Contact your child's nursery or school – If you want to find out more about reading with your child, request time to talk to your child's teacher.

Join the local library – Local libraries are a great source of books, tapes, videos and CDs for children of all ages, and they are free. Address: see your local telephone directory or contact the national Library Association, CILIP.
Tel: 020 7255 0500. www.cilip.org.uk

Booktrust offers advice on sharing books and produces a wide range of lists for babies, picture story books (for 2–6 years), beginning to read (5–8 years), newly fluent readers (6–10 years). Address: Book House, 45 East Hill, London, SW18 2QZ
Tel: 020 8516 2977. www.booktrust.org.uk

Directgov includes a section for parents that provides information on health and safety, preschool, childcare and legal information.
www.direct.gov.uk/en/Parents/index.htm

The National Literacy Trust gives advice to parents helping their pre-school children with reading.
Address: 68 South Lambeth Road, London, SW8 1RL
Tel: 020 7587 1842. www.literacytrust.org.uk

The Federation of Children's Book Groups can provide you with free booklists.
Address: 2 Bridge Wood View, Horsforth, Leeds, LS18 5PE
Tel: 0113 258 8910. www.fcbg.org.uk

The British Dyslexia Association can provide advice if your child has specific reading difficulties.
Address: Unit 8, Bracknell Beeches, Old Bracknell Lane, Bracknell, RG12 7BW
Tel: 0845 251 9002 (Helpline) 0845 251 9003 (Administration)
www.bdadyslexia.org.uk

The National Childminding Association promotes quality, registered childminding to enable children to be cared for and learn in their own homes.
Address: NCMA, Royal Court, 81 Tweedy Road, Bromley, Kent, BR1 1TG
Tel: 0800 169 4486. www.ncma.org.uk

Mantra Lingua Ltd publishes a range of bilingual children's books and resources in different languages.
Address: Global House, 303 Ballards Lane, London, NW12 8NP
Tel: 020 8845 5123. www.mantralingua.com

National Centre for Language and Literacy has a range of publications aimed at parents about aspects of reading, language and literacy.
Address: The University of Reading, Bulmershe Court, Reading, RG6 1HY
Tel: 0118 378 8820. www.ncll.org.uk

Talk To Your Baby is a campaign run by the National Literacy Trust to encourage parents and carers to talk more to children from birth to age three.
Tel: 020 7820 6265. www.literacytrust.org.uk/talktoyourbaby

Walker Books include pages on their website offering advice to parents and carers about choosing books and reading together from birth onwards.
Address: 87 Vauxhall Walk, London, SE11 5HJ
Tel: 020 7793 0909. www.walker.co.uk

We would like to thank **Madeleine Lindley Ltd,** suppliers of children's books to teachers and practitioners, for allowing us to browse their extensive book collections and work on their premises, and for offering advice.
Address: Book Centre, Broadwalk, Broadway Business Park, Oldham, OL9 9XA
Tel: 0161 683 4400. www.madeleinelindley.com

Contact details

For further information on all of our books please go to:

http://shop.niace.org.uk

For further copies of this book contact:

NIACE Publications
PO Box 170
Ashford
TN24 0ZX

Or call: 0870 600 2400

promoting adult learning

www.niace.org.uk
ISBN: 978 1 86201 437 4